S0-DGI-111

Knights

Rachel Firth

Designed by Lucy Owen

with Glen Bird and Helen Wood

Edited by Jane Chisholm and Gillian Doherty

Illustrated by Giacinto Gaudenzi, Dominic Groebner, Massimiliano Longo and Glen Bird

Consultants: Dr. Charles Insley and Professor John France

Contents

Internet links

Look for the Internet links boxes throughout this book. They contain descriptions of Web sites where you can find out more about knights. For links to these Web sites, go to **www.usborne-quicklinks.com** and type in the keywords "discovery knights".

Next to some of the pictures in the book you will see a star symbol. Wherever you see one of these, it means that you can download the picture from the **Usborne Quicklinks Web site**. For more information on using the Internet, and downloading Usborne pictures, see inside the back cover and page 47.

Cover picture: a suit of plate armour
Title page: a medieval picture of two knights fighting with lances.
This page: a section of the Bayeux tapestry showing Norman knights fighting Saxon knights

What were knights? ....

Knights were soldiers who fought on horseback. Some of the most famous knights lived in Europe during a time known as the Middle Ages (about 1000–1550). For most of that time they were the most formidable force on the battlefield.

Who became knights?

At first, almost any man could become a knight if he had been trained and could afford to buy armour and horses. Later, only the sons of important, rich men called nobles could be knighted.

Armoured warriors

Knights were fearsome fighting machines. They wore protective metal clothing, called armour, and carried huge, heavy swords. Horses were also an essential part of a knight's equipment. Most knights had three — one for fighting on, one for travelling on and one for carrying luggage.

Internet links

For a link to a Web site where you can take a guided tour of the Middle Ages, go to
www.usborne-quicklinks.com

This knight and horse are in full armour. Horse armour was very expensive and only the richest knights could afford it.

Knight symbols

Knights carried shields for protection and wore spiky pieces of metal, called spurs, on their shoes to control their horses. Spurs and swords were important symbols of knighthood. When someone became a knight, he was given spurs and a sword, and if these were taken away from him, it meant that he was no longer a knight.

Shields were made of wood and most were decorated with patterns and pictures.

This part of the spur was worn around the knight's ankle.

The spiky parts of spurs were pressed into a horse's sides to spur it on to move faster.

Most swords were made from iron or steel. Some were so big they needed to be held with two hands.

Legendary knights

There are many stories about knights and their adventures. The most famous ones are about King Arthur and his knights. According to legend, Arthur's knights fought monsters and rescued maidens. Many people think that Arthur and his knights really existed and lived in the 5th or 6th century.

This medieval picture shows some of the adventures of Sir Lancelot, one of King Arthur's knights.

Fact: Only men were allowed to become knights. They were all addressed as "Sir".

Deadly weapons

Guns weren't invented until the end of the Middle Ages, but knights had plenty of other lethal weapons, which they used to fight in hand-to-hand combat with their enemies. Their main weapons were swords and lances.

Slashing swords

Knights usually fought with large, double-edged swords. The most common type was called a hand-and-a-half sword. It was short and light enough to be used one-handed, but it had an extra-long handle, which meant that it was possible to use it two-handed as well.

Sharp points

Knights also fought with smaller, lighter swords with very sharp points. These were slim enough to slip through gaps in an enemy's armour and helmet, causing terrible injuries to his joints and head. Some of these types of swords could even pierce armour.

This knight is using a 1m (3ft) two-handed sword.

Internet links

For a link to a Web site where you can find out more about medieval weapons, go to **www.usborne-quicklinks.com**

Long lances

A lance was a long wooden pole with a sharp metal tip at one end. Knights mainly used them when fighting on horseback. They enabled them to attack enemy soldiers without having to get off their horses or get too close.

From handle to tip this lance is 4m (13ft) long. It has a guard, called a vamplate, to protect the hand.

Striking axes

Battle axes could be used to strike enemies down at close range or hurled at them from a distance. War hammers were short-handled axes with a blade on one side and a curved spike on the other. Knights used them while on horseback. On foot, they used long-handled axes, called pollaxes, to attack mounted knights from the ground.

This is a type of pollaxe called a halberd. The curved spike on the right of the pole was used to pull knights off their horses.

This double-headed battle axe is made from iron and has razor-sharp edges.

Maces and flails

Maces were short sticks with heavy metal ends, which could crush a knight's body inside his armour. Some maces had one or more spiky iron balls attached to their handles by chains. These were known as flails. They were capable of piercing a knight's armour and smashing his bones.

Flanged, or ridged, maces like this one were widely used from the 13th century onwards.

The ball on this flail is attached to the handle by a 30cm (1ft) chain.

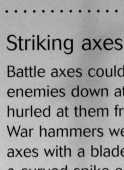

Fact: Many knights thought that archers were cowardly because they shot their weapons from a long way away rather than engaging in hand-to-hand combat.

Chain mail and shields

rmour was essential if a knight was to survive a battle. With the help of a shield, which was used to fend off heavy blows, it gave a knight good protection against most weapons. Designs changed throughout the Middle Ages. On these two pages, you can read about some of the earlier ones.

Chain mail

Early medieval armour was made from thousands of little iron rings linked together. This is called chain mail. Knights wore chain mail shirts, called hauberks, together with leggings, called greaves, made from chain mail or leather.

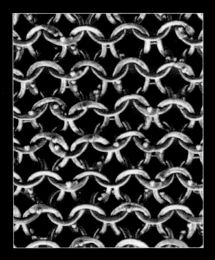

This is a close-up picture of chain mail. It took about two thousand of these iron rings to make a single shirt.

This man is wearing a 12th-century style suit of chain mail.

The chain mail hood, or coif, protects the neck and head. A helmet was usually worn over it.

The cloth tunic worn over the chain mail is called a surcoat. It's for decoration rather than protection.

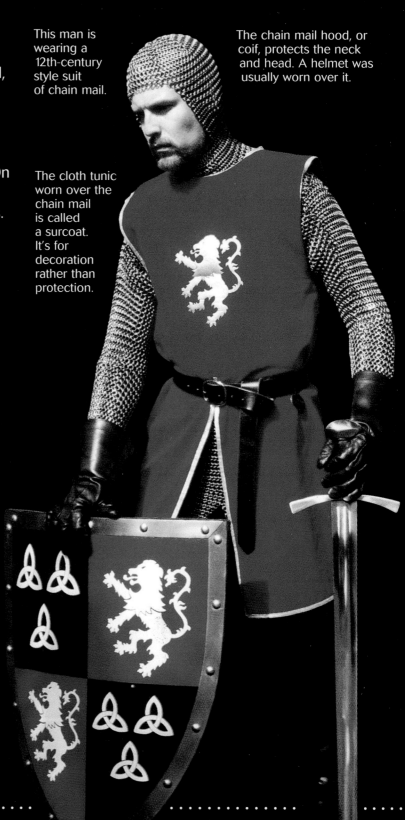

This is a section of the Bayeux tapestry, an 11th-century tapestry which illustrates the Norman invasion of England in 1066. The knights shown are wearing knee-length hauberks and pointed helmets.

Extra protection

Chain mail could protect knights from slashing swords, but not from heavy blows which could break their bones. For extra protection, knights wore padded vests, called arming jackets, under their chain mail.

A blow to the head could easily kill a person, so knights wore helmets, as well as chain mail hoods and padded caps. Early helmets had pointed or rounded tops. Some had bars, called nasals, to protect the nose, but the rest of the face was left unprotected.

Internet links

For a link to a Web site where you can find a gallery of medieval armour, go to **www.usborne-quicklinks.com**

Shields

Early medieval shields were almost as big as the knights who carried them. They were made from lightweight wood and were usually kite-shaped. Later ones were much smaller. This was because knights had better armour and didn't need such big shields to protect them.

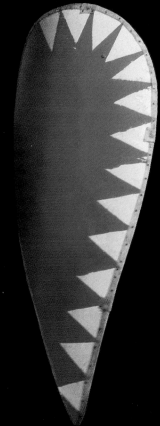

An early medieval kite-shaped shield

Fact: Chain mail rusted very easily, so it had to be rolled in sand regularly to keep it clean.

Plate armour

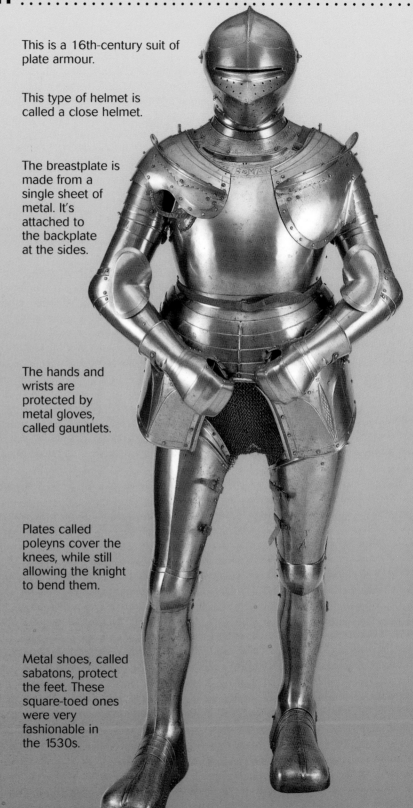

As more deadly weapons were invented, knights needed armour that gave them better protection. They began to replace some of their chain mail with parts made from metal sheets. By the end of the Middle Ages, knights were wearing armour made almost entirely from metal sheets joined together. This sort of armour was called plate armour.

Moving joints

Knights needed to be able to bend their arms and legs while wearing armour. Plate armour covering a knight's joints was made of lots of overlapping pieces. These were joined together loosely so that when the knight moved the plates could move with him.

Here you can see the overlapping strips that made up a metal glove. They are joined together by rivets which allowed the strips to move.

Rivet

This is a 16th-century suit of plate armour.

This type of helmet is called a close helmet.

The breastplate is made from a single sheet of metal. It's attached to the backplate at the sides.

The hands and wrists are protected by metal gloves, called gauntlets.

Plates called poleyns cover the knees, while still allowing the knight to bend them.

Metal shoes, called sabatons, protect the feet. These square-toed ones were very fashionable in the 1530s.

Head cover

Late-medieval helmets completely covered the head, face and neck. The part that protected the face was called a visor. It had slits and holes so that the knight could see out and breathe. Some visors were attached to the helmet with hinges and could be lifted up when the knight wasn't fighting.

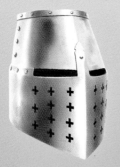

A 12th-century Great Helm with a fixed visor

A 14th-century bascinet helmet with no visor

A 14th-century bascinet with a fixed visor

★ Here you can see how a visor lifted up. This helmet also has a chain mail collar, or coif, attached to its base.

A better fit

Plate armour was more comfortable to wear than chain mail. Although both types of armour weighed about the same, plate armour felt lighter because its weight rested more evenly over the knight's body. Knights bought their armour from skilled craftsmen. The highest quality armour was made from parts that were specially moulded to fit the knight who was going to wear it.

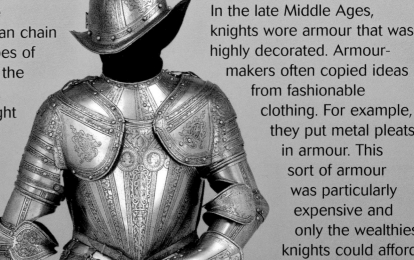

Fashionable armour

In the late Middle Ages, knights wore armour that was highly decorated. Armour-makers often copied ideas from fashionable clothing. For example, they put metal pleats in armour. This sort of armour was particularly expensive and only the wealthiest knights could afford to keep up with the latest fashions.

Finely-decorated armour like this was the height of fashion in late-medieval Italy.

Fact: The heaviest suits of plate armour weighed about 23kg (50lb). That's as heavy as about fifty cans of baked beans.

Knights and castles

Knights and other nobles lived in castles along with their families and servants. Castles were strong buildings that were designed to protect people inside from attacks from outside. Most castles had a team of knights and other soldiers, known as a garrison, ready to defend it if it was attacked.

Early castles

Some of the earliest castles were made of wood and were called motte and bailey castles. The motte was a hill with a wooden tower built on top of it. At the foot of the motte was the bailey, where most of the people of the castle lived. The two parts were connected by a drawbridge. If the castle was attacked, people could climb up to the safety of the motte and lift up the bridge, so that no one could cross it after them.

The motte and bailey castle in this diagram is surrounded by a wooden fence to help prevent enemy soldiers getting inside.

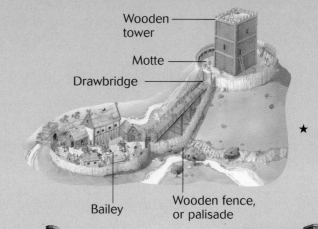

Wooden tower

Motte

Drawbridge

Bailey

Wooden fence, or palisade

Fact: It could take ten years for 2,000 workers to build a castle.

Walls and keeps

If they could afford the materials, people built stone castles, which were much stronger and safer. The earliest ones just consisted of a large thick-walled tower, called a keep. Later ones had an extra wall around the keep. Later still, people got rid of keeps altogether and just had walls with towers surrounding a courtyard.

Bodiam Castle is an example of a castle built around a courtyard. It's surrounded by a wide water-filled ditch, called a moat, for extra protection.

Concentric castles

By the 13th century, castles in Britain were being built with rings of walls, one inside another. These are known as concentric castles. The outer walls were lower than the inner walls. This meant that soldiers on the inner walls could fire arrows at enemies outside the castle without injuring soldiers on the outer walls.

A diagram of a concentric castle from above

Moat

Tower

Inner wall

Gatehouse

Main gatehouse with drawbridge

Outer wall

Medieval warfare

Wars were happening all the time in the Middle Ages. They could be anything from local disagreements between rival nobles to full-scale wars between countries trying to take land off each other. The most common types of warfare were raids, battles and sieges.

Knights and armies

Knights made up about a fifth of a medieval army. The rest were foot soldiers. Some of these were archers, who fought with bows and arrows; others fought with long lance-like weapons called pikes. Knights usually fought on horseback, but were sometimes ordered to dismount and fight on foot.

Destructive raids

Raids were surprise attacks on an enemy. The aim was to destroy their supplies and property, making it difficult for them to fight. During a raid, soldiers stole people's possessions, and burned whole villages and towns to the ground. Anyone who got in their way was killed, and many other people starved to death because all their food had been taken or destroyed.

Internet links

For a link to a Web site where you can find out about the Battle of Hastings and play a game, go to www.usborne-quicklinks.com

Most battles were chaotic and extremely violent, and many soldiers died from being trampled, rather than from sword or pike injuries.

Battle tactics

Battles were big fights between enemy armies. They didn't happen very often because whole armies could be killed during a battle and commanders didn't want to risk this.

Traditionally, the most important part of the battle was when knights from opposing sides led the attack by charging towards each other on horseback. But armies sometimes used defensive tactics to prevent this. For example, they might put sharp stakes in the ground to injure charging horses and stop knights from advancing.

Soldiers drove stakes into the ground to pierce horses' bellies if they tried to jump over them. ★

Capturing castles

Sieges were attempts to capture a castle or town. By doing this, an army gained a new base from which to fight, and won control of the surrounding land. You can find out more about sieges on pages 16–21.

Fact: In a battle or siege, archers could shoot arrows at a rate of 12 a minute.

Under siege ....

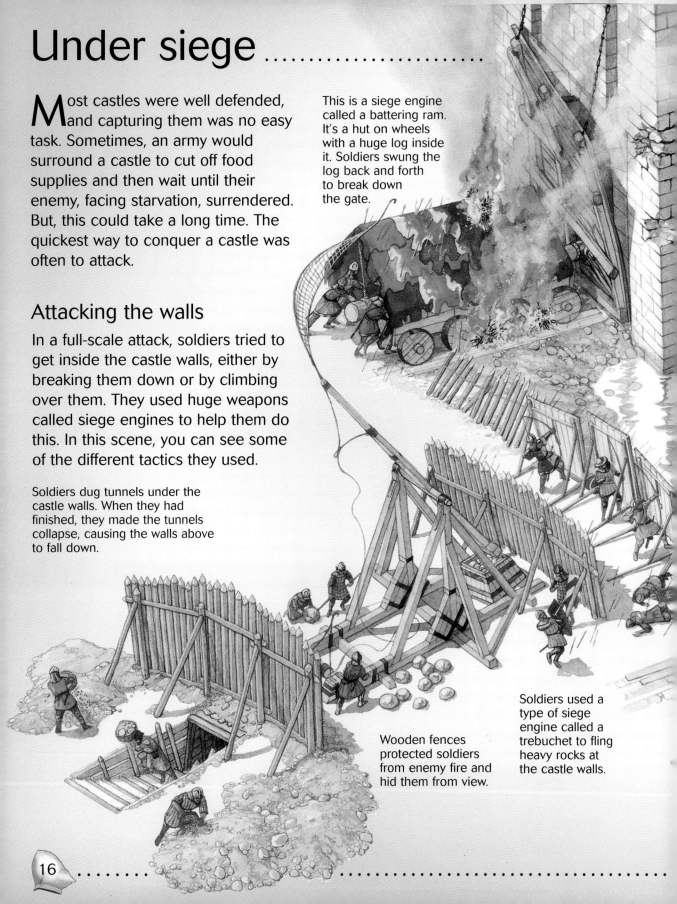

ost castles were well defended, and capturing them was no easy task. Sometimes, an army would surround a castle to cut off food supplies and then wait until their enemy, facing starvation, surrendered. But, this could take a long time. The quickest way to conquer a castle was often to attack.

Attacking the walls

In a full-scale attack, soldiers tried to get inside the castle walls, either by breaking them down or by climbing over them. They used huge weapons called siege engines to help them do this. In this scene, you can see some of the different tactics they used.

Soldiers dug tunnels under the castle walls. When they had finished, they made the tunnels collapse, causing the walls above to fall down.

This is a siege engine called a battering ram. It's a hut on wheels with a huge log inside it. Soldiers swung the log back and forth to break down the gate.

Wooden fences protected soldiers from enemy fire and hid them from view.

Soldiers used a type of siege engine called a trebuchet to fling heavy rocks at the castle walls.

Attacking soldiers used tall, wooden siege towers to help them climb over the castle walls. To get the towers close enough to the castle, they had to fill in part of the moat.

Defending soldiers used long poles with hooks to push away scaling ladders as attacking soldiers climbed up them.

Fact: Enemies sometimes got into a castle by devious means, for example, by bribing a guard to open a gate, or climbing up the castle's drains.

Weapons of attack

Siege engines and other large weapons were crucial if an army was to succeed in capturing a castle. The most effective of these weapons were ones that could bombard castles and the people inside with missiles.

Huge catapults

One of the most destructive types of siege engine was the trebuchet. It had a sling at one end and a weight at the other, and it worked like a giant catapult. The most powerful trebuchets could hurl missiles weighing as much as 270kg (600lb), which is about the same weight as a cow.

Internet links

For a link to a Web site where you can build a trebuchet online and try to destroy a castle with it, go to **www.usborne-quicklinks.com**

This 13th-century trebuchet could fling missiles over a distance of about 300m (1,000ft).

The wooden box at this end of the trebuchet's arm is the weight. It was filled with earth, sand, stones or lead.

Missiles, such as heavy stones, were loaded into the sling at the end of the trebuchet's arm.

These pictures show how a trebuchet worked.

Soldiers pulled the sling down and attached it to a hook. They then loaded the missile and pulled the arm up using ropes and a winding wheel.

Next, they hit the hook to release the arm and the weight. The force of the weight dropping made the sling fly up, sending the missile into the air.

Giant crossbows

Ballistas were giant crossbows which shot huge, iron-tipped wooden arrows over distances of up to 400m (1,300ft). Ballistas were easier to move around than trebuchets and took up much less room. But they couldn't do as much damage to castle walls. They were mainly used to kill enemy soldiers – a single arrow could go through several people in one shot.

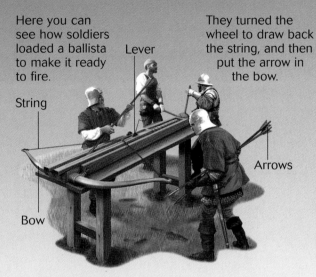

Here you can see how soldiers loaded a ballista to make it ready to fire.

They turned the wheel to draw back the string, and then put the arrow in the bow.

Lever

String

Arrows

Bow

When the string was tight, they pulled back the lever to fire the arrow. ★

Cannon power

From the 1300s onwards, soldiers began to use cannons to fire stone or iron balls. Cannons were fired using gunpowder. This was packed into the cannon, and the cannon ball was dropped on top of it. The gunpowder was then lit, causing it to explode and force the cannon ball out of the cannon at high speed.

Gunpowder gave cannons the power to fire heavier missiles and do much more damage than siege engines. But cannons were unreliable and could explode when fired.

This huge 15th-century cannon was so heavy it took about a hundred men to move it.

Fact: Sometimes, attackers used trebuchets to toss dead animals or manure into castles, to spread disease among the enemy.

Fighting back

Castles were built to withstand heavy attacks and were designed to make it easy for soldiers inside to fight back, without making themselves vulnerable to enemy fire.

In this scene, you can see some of the different tactics soldiers used to defend their castle.

Shooting at the enemy

Castle walls had slits, called arrow loops, that were wider on the inside than on the outside. Soldiers inside could easily fire arrows out of them. But the slits were too narrow to shoot through from the outside. This meant that soldiers inside could fire arrows out without fear of being shot.

Dropping missiles

During sieges, people often built wooden hoardings that stuck out over the castle walls. They had holes in them for dropping missiles through onto the enemy below. Some castles had permanent, stone versions of these, called machicolations.

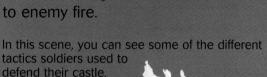

Soldiers poured burning liquid onto attackers trying to climb the walls.

Archers fired arrows through arrow loops, at enemy soldiers at the base of the walls.

Gaps in the castle's battlements gave archers a wide range of fire.

Soldiers threw hot sand and stones through holes in the towers.

In this photograph of a gatehouse, you can clearly see several rectangular murder holes in the ceiling.

Murder holes

Some castles had holes known as murder holes above the gates. Soldiers could pour boiling water or hot sand through them onto enemy soldiers who broke into the gatehouse. They could also pour cold water through them to put out fires started by the enemy.

Throwing fire

During some sieges, soldiers used a burning liquid called "Greek fire" to try to set fire to their attackers' siege towers. No one is certain what it was made from, but it burned ferociously, even on water, and was very difficult to put out. It also stuck to anything it came into contact with, including people.

Becoming a knight

It could take as long as 15 years to become a knight. Future knights started training at the age of six or seven. When they reached about 21, if they had learned to fight well and could afford all the equipment they needed, they could be knighted.

Pages were expected to serve meals to their lord and lady.

Pages

Very young trainee knights were called pages. They were sent away from home to train in a knight's castle. There they learned basic fighting skills and were taught simple household skills and how to behave in a castle.

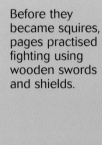

Some pages learned to read and write as part of their training.

Before they became squires, pages practised fighting using wooden swords and shields.

Learning to fight

When a page was about 14, he moved on to the next stage in his training and became a squire. Groups of squires lived and trained together, and learned to fight using real weapons.

Squires practised hitting targets called quintains with a lance.

To get used to heavy armour, squires ran around in it.

Squires were responsible for looking after their lord's horses.

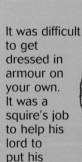

It was difficult to get dressed in armour on your own. It was a squire's job to help his lord to put his armour on.

Being knighted

Only the king or another knight could make a squire into a knight. This usually happened in a ceremony called an accolade. The pictures below show some of the things that happened before and during the ceremony.

Internet links

For a link to a Web site where you can try online activities about a knight's life, go to **www.usborne-quicklinks.com**

The squire spent the night before the ceremony praying that he would be a good knight.

The king knighted the squire by tapping him on the shoulders and head with a sword.

The new knight received a sword and spurs as signs that he was now a knight.

Celebration time

After a squire was knighted there were often celebrations. Knights took part in fighting competitions, called tournaments, and there were feasts, music and dancing for everyone. These celebrations often lasted for days.

Knighted on the battlefield

Not everyone was knighted with such ceremony. Squires were sometimes quickly knighted before a battle to give them courage, or after a battle as a reward for being exceptionally brave.

This medieval painting shows King Richard II of England knighting someone just before a battle.

Fact: Some squires stayed squires all their lives because they couldn't afford to buy their own armour and horses.

Tournaments

Knights fought even when they were not at war. They held tournaments to give them a chance to practise and show off their battle skills and to help to train young knights for battle. Tournaments were made up of several types of event.

Knights wore bright colours during tournaments to make them stand out.

Jousts

A joust was a form of one-to-one combat between two knights on horseback. Armed with lances, they galloped down tracks called lists. As they passed one another, each used his lance to try to hit his opponent. Knights could score points, depending on how and where they hit their opponents.

The knight on the left would score two points out of three for hitting his opponent's shield like this.

For breaking his lance tip on the other knight's lance, a knight would lose points.

Maximum points were scored for knocking your opponent off his horse.

Mock battles

In this painting, groups of knights all fight at once in a mock battle. Ladies watch from the safety of a raised box.

Mock battles, known as mêlées, were the earliest type of tournament. Originally, they were violent, disorganized fights between groups of knights, using real weapons. In later mêlées, knights divided into two fighting teams, and each side tried to capture as many prisoners from the other as possible.

Internet links

For a link to a Web site where you can find out more about tournaments and how to joust, go to **www.usborne-quicklinks.com**

Pas d'armes

In an event called a pas d'armes, a knight or team of knights chose a place to defend, such as a road or bridge, and challenged other knights to fight. Pas d'armes were usually friendly events. Knights were expected to show good manners as well as good fighting skills.

Running the rings

Not all competitions at tournaments involved fighting. In an event called "running the rings", knights competed with one another to spear small targets with their lances, while riding their horses at a gallop. The competition was a test of accuracy and good horsemanship.

The knight had to steer his horse and aim very carefully to catch such small hoops on his lance.

Fact: At one very violent tournament held in the German town of Neuss, in 1241, about eighty knights and squires were killed in a mock battle.

25

Coats of arms

It could be very difficult to recognize knights when they were dressed in full armour. To overcome this problem, they had colours, patterns and pictures painted on their shields. These are called coats of arms. No two people could have the same coat of arms.

This knight is dressed for a tournament. His distinctive coat of arms makes it very easy for the judges to recognize him.

Describing arms

Special terms, known as blazonry, are used to describe coats of arms. For example, the word *argent* is used for "silver", and *rampant* for "things standing up". The terms come from an ancient version of the French language.

Internet links

For a link to a Web site where you can find out more about how coats of arms are designed, go to **www.usborne-quicklinks.com**

Colours and symbols

Colours and pictures on coats of arms sometimes had meanings. These varied from one country and period of time to another. For example, a cat could stand for freedom or courage. Some coats of arms reflected the names of the knights who wore them. So a knight called Trumpington might have trumpets on his coat of arms.

Here are some examples of the meanings of symbols and colours on a selection of coats of arms.

Bear: strength or cunning

Blue, or azure, background: truth

Bee: efficiency

Dragon: protection or bravery

Red, or gules, background: strength

Gold background: generosity

Daggers: justice or honour

Moons: power

Unicorn: courage

Black, or sable, background: grief

Lion (rampant): strength or bravery

Choosing arms

At first, a knight could choose to have any design he wanted on his coat of arms, but a strict set of rules soon developed. For example, knights weren't allowed to have gold or silver symbols on gold or silver backgrounds. In England, by 1424, if a knight wanted to have a new coat of arms, he had to have it approved by an organization called the College of Arms.

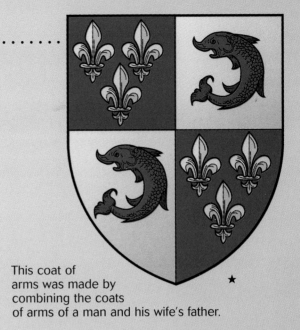

This coat of arms was made by combining the coats of arms of a man and his wife's father. ★

Father to son

Coats of arms could be inherited. This meant that when a knight died his coat of arms passed on to his eldest living son. A knight's sons could wear their father's coat of arms while he was still alive, provided they added marks, called marks of cadency, to it to indicate their place in the family. When the knight died, the eldest son was allowed to remove his mark and fully inherit his father's coat of arms.

These are some examples of the marks of cadency that knights' sons added to coats of arms in late medieval England.

Eldest son	Second son	Third son	Fourth son	Fifth son

Sixth son	Seventh son	Eighth son	Ninth son ★

Combining arms

Most women didn't have their own coats of arms, but could wear their father's or husband's. Sometimes, when a woman married she combined her father's coat of arms with her husband's, to make a new one. This is known as marshalling. There are different ways of doing this.

This way of combining arms is called dimidation. The coats of arms have been split vertically and joined together.

Fact: If a knight had no sons, his daughter could inherit his coat of arms. She was known as a heraldic heiress.

27

Heralds

By the end of the Middle Ages, there were many different coats of arms, often with complicated pictures and symbols on them. People called heralds were trained to recognize all the different ones.

Training to be a herald

Trainee heralds were called pursuivants. As well as learning to recognize all the different coats of arms, they had to memorize the family history behind each of them, and learn the different terms used to describe them. The most senior heralds were known as Kings of Arms. They were the people who gave knights permission to use coats of arms and advised them on which designs to choose.

In some countries, you could tell pursuivants and heralds apart by the way they wore their shirts, or tabards.

Heralds wore their tabards with the openings at the sides

Pursuivants wore their tabards sideways, with the large panels draped over their arms.

Heralds at tournaments

This medieval picture shows a herald announcing the start of a tournament.

Knowing about coats of arms made heralds very useful at tournaments. As they were the only ones who could identify all the contestants, it was their job to note how many points each knight scored. Wealthy knights hired their own heralds to introduce them as they rode out onto the field. The herald shouted out his knight's name and titles, and boasted about how good he was at fighting.

Internet links

For a link to a Web site where you can play a heraldry game and learn more about coats of arms, go to **www.usborne-quicklinks.com**

Fact: Heralds still train and work today in the United Kingdom, at the College of Arms.

Heralds at war

During times of war, knights who had heralds took them with them to the battlefield. Some heralds acted as messengers between the two sides. They had to follow strict rules and were not allowed to work as spies. This meant that they weren't supposed to tell their side any secrets about their enemy's preparations, although they probably broke this rule from time to time.

Rolls of arms

Heralds made lists, called rolls of arms, of everyone taking part in a battle or tournament. They did this by writing descriptions of the coats of arms or by painting copies of them. Rolls of arms are the only records we have of some of the earlier coats of arms.

This is a picture of part of a roll of arms. The entire roll records 324 different coats of arms from the 15th century.

This is a herald's tabard, decorated with a coat of arms. Heralds wore them on the battlefield to make sure that they would not be mistaken for soldiers and killed.

Counting the dead

Heralds watched battles from a distance and used their knowledge of coats of arms to note down anyone who was behaving in a cowardly way. It was also a herald's job to record his knight's last wishes, in case he didn't survive the battle. When the battle was over, the heralds counted the dead nobles and identified them.

Hunting and games

Hunting was one of the most popular activities for knights. They did it both for fun and to provide fresh meat for their families to eat. Knights hunted large animals, such as foxes and deer, on horseback, and small ones, such as rabbits and hares, on foot using birds.

Hunting on horseback

When hunting on horseback, knights used dogs to help them track down the animals. The dogs were trained to detect the animals' scents. Sometimes, knights paid peasants to run ahead and make lots of noise. This frightened the animals out of their hiding places.

Sport of nobles

Knights hunted in forests set aside especially for hunting. Only people from noble families were allowed to hunt there, which meant that there were always plenty of animals for them to hunt. If peasants were caught hunting, they were severely punished – they could have a hand cut off, or even be killed.

Internet links

For a link to a Web site where you can listen to a falcon and see a video of a falcon as it hunts, go to **www.usborne-quicklinks.com**

In this medieval painting, a knight on horseback is chasing a stag. He carries a spear ready to stab it as soon as he is close enough.

Hunting with birds

Hunting with birds of prey (birds that hunt and eat other animals) was one of the most popular sports in the Middle Ages. People caught wild birds while they were still young, and trained them to catch and kill small animals without eating them. The type of bird you were allowed to use depended on how important you were. People were severely punished if they were caught hunting with the wrong sort of bird.

Only emperors hunted with eagles.

Kings hunted with gyrfalcons.

Princes hunted with peregrine falcons.

Knights hunted with sakers.

Squires hunted with lanner falcons.

Ladies hunted with merlins.

Other games

Knights enjoyed playing card games, board games and games with dice. Chess was particularly popular, and knights and other nobles often held competitions with prizes for the winners. They also played a complicated version of noughts and crosses, called Merrelles, or Nine Men's Morris.

These chess pieces were made in Scandinavia in the 12th century.

This medieval picture shows people playing a game of dice. Dice was very popular with peasants as well as with knights.

Chivalry

People expected knights to have very high standards of behaviour. For example, they were supposed to be brave, loyal, generous and truthful at all times. These ideas about how knights should behave were known as the code of chivalry.

Courtly love

Knights were expected to treat noblewomen with great respect. A knight who loved a lady was supposed to be humble, faithful and entirely devoted to her. Knights tried to impress their ladies, without expecting any sign of affection in return. This way of treating ladies was known as courtly love.

On this medieval shield, the knight is shown kneeling humbly before his lady.

Aiming to impress

Some knights tried to win the love of their ladies by winning tournaments. Others went to far greater lengths. For example, Ulrich von Lichtenstein, an Austrian knight, travelled around Europe wearing the figure of Venus, the goddess of love, on his helmet. Wherever he went, he jousted with other knights in the hope that this would impress his lady.

This is a medieval painting of Ulrich von Lichtenstein. He travelled all the way from Austria to Venice dressed like this, challenging other knights along the way.

Internet links

For a link to a Web site where you can read about medieval ideas of chivalry, go to **www.usborne-quicklinks.com**

Fact: The word "chivalry" comes from the French word for knight – "chevalier".

On the battlefield

Being chivalrous on the battlefield meant fighting fiercely and bravely. But it also meant treating enemy knights with respect. The code of chivalry allowed a knight to surrender without losing his fellow knights' respect. If a knight gave himself up in this way, he could expect to be treated well by his enemy until the time of his release.

Troubadours

Stories about chivalry were very popular in the Middle Ages. Early medieval poems were called *chansons de geste* which means "songs of deeds". They were mainly about the heroic adventures and chivalrous deeds of knights.

Later, poets called troubadours wrote about love and romances between ladies and knights. Many troubadours became famous, and read their poems in royal castles.

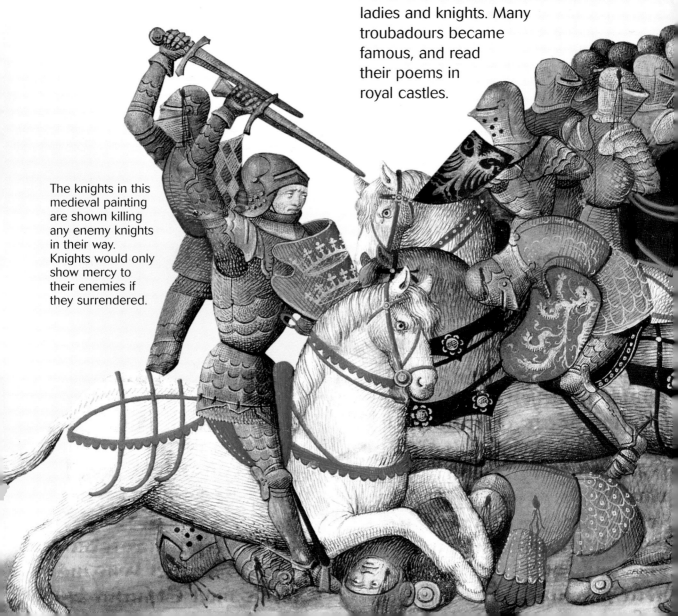

The knights in this medieval painting are shown killing any enemy knights in their way. Knights would only show mercy to their enemies if they surrendered.

The Crusades

(intro)

Many knights fought in a series of religious campaigns called the Crusades. During the Crusades, two sides — Muslims from the Middle East and European Christians — fought each other because they both wanted control of an area in the Middle East known as the Holy Land.

This medieval illustration shows a knight kneeling in prayer as he promises to go to fight in the Crusades.

How it all started

The Holy Land was important to Christians because it was where Jesus lived and died. For many centuries, the Muslim rulers of the area allowed Christians to travel there to pray. But, in the late 11th century, new Muslim rulers, Seljuk Turks, took over and began to threaten and attack the Christians. In response, the Christian Church declared a holy war, or crusade, against the Muslims.

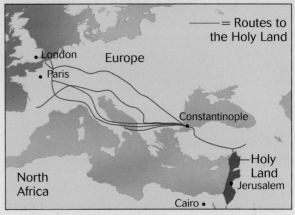

It took some knights as long as 11 months, riding on horseback, to get from Europe to the Holy Land. Here you can see some of the routes they took.

Land of opportunity

About 30,000 knights and soldiers went to fight in the First Crusade. Many fought to prove that they were good Christians, but some had other motives. Some poorer knights, who had no land of their own, hoped to win land and riches from their enemies if they defeated them in battle.

Taking control

In 1099, the Christians took control of Jerusalem, the most important city in the Holy Land, and won the First Crusade. But, in 1187, under their leader Saladin, the Muslims won it back again. There were a further seven crusades over the next 200 years, but the Christians never got Jerusalem back.

Crusaders fighting Muslims during the Third Crusade

A medieval picture of Saladin, leader of the Muslims in the Holy land from 1171–1193

New knowledge

In spite of all the fighting, contact between Christians and Muslims brought benefits for both groups. Muslims learned new battle tactics from the Christians, while the Christians learned much from the Muslims about science and music.

Internet links

For a link to a Web site where you can find out about the Crusades, go to **www.usborne-quicklinks.com**

Fact: Among the many new things crusaders brought from the Middle East to Europe were magnetic compasses, lutes (a kind of musical instrument) and paper.

Templars and Hospitallers

After the First Crusade, some knights stayed on in the Holy Land and formed religious groups, or orders, of monks. They lived religious lives but, unlike other monks, they were also prepared to fight for their religion. Two of the most important of these orders were the Knights Templar and the Knights Hospitaller.

Protecting visitors

The Knights Templar protected and guided Christians visiting the Holy Land. They were also a much feared and respected fighting force. When a knight became a Templar, he took many religious vows, including a promise to live a life of poverty. But many wealthy nobles gave the order money, and the Templars soon became rich and powerful, building up a vast store of treasure.

Wealth and power

The Templars used their money to set up some of the first banks. They also owned the biggest fleet of ships in Europe and built magnificent castles all over the Holy Land. But their wealth and power came to an abrupt end in 1312. The Church accused them of holding non-Christian beliefs and they were disbanded. Many thousands of them were arrested and killed, and all of their treasure mysteriously disappeared.

This picture of two Templars sharing a horse is meant to show that they are too poor for each to have a horse of his own.

Medical monks

The Knights Hospitaller looked after sick Christians in Jerusalem. Like the Templars, they became skilled fighters, and built spectacular castles, but continued to run their hospitals at the same time. With their large fleet of ships, they improved trade between the Holy Land and Europe, and helped to control pirates in the area.

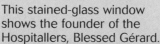

This stained-glass window shows the founder of the Hospitallers, Blessed Gérard.

This is Krak des Chevaliers, one of the biggest Hospitaller castles in the Holy Land.

Hospitallers today

The Hospitallers were eventually forced to leave the Holy Land by the Muslims. They moved to Rhodes and then Malta, but were disbanded in the 16th century. In the 19th century, the order was revived and exists today as the Order of of St. John. They no longer fight, but they do still care for the sick. They have a hospital in Jerusalem and run the St. John Ambulance organization.

A late medieval coin with the Maltese Cross on it – the symbol of the Order of St. John

The modern badge of the St. John Ambulance organization

Noblewomen

The daughters and wives of knights generally had much less freedom than their fathers and husbands. Noblewomen were expected to marry young, to have and raise lots of children and to help run their husbands' castles.

Internet links

For a link to a Web site where you can find out more about Joan of Arc, go to
www.usborne-quicklinks.com

Ladies of the castle

In this medieval painting, the women are going hunting. They had to sit sideways on their saddles to be able to ride in their long dresses.

A knight's wife organized the servants and made sure that cooking, brewing and other household jobs were done properly. In their spare time, ladies of the castle played musical instruments, embroidered, went hunting and played games such as chess.

Home alone

Knights spent a lot of time away from their castles, fighting in wars. At these times, it was a wife's duty to look after the castle, and hire and fire servants. If the castle came under attack, the lady of the castle was even expected to organize its defence.

This 14th-century painting shows a French noblewoman wearing ornate clothing. The servants of noblewomen would have helped them to dress.

Medieval fashion

Noblewomen dressed in expensive materials, such as silk or fur. They decorated their clothes with jewels and wore their hair in nets made of silver or gold thread. Later, it became fashionable for noblewomen to wear headdresses which completely covered their hair.

Here are some examples of different medieval headdresses.

A rolled headdress

A hennin headdress

A butterfly headdress

Famous women

Although many medieval women's lives were restricted compared to the lives of most women today, some became very successful and influential. They worked as doctors, ran businesses, wrote books and even went to war.

This is a picture of Joan of Arc, a French woman who led her country's armies into battle against the English in 1429.

A painting of Christine de Pisan, a famous medieval writer, presenting one of her books to Princess Isabel of Bavaria

Fact: Many medieval women married when they were only 12 years old. Once a woman was married, all her possessions became the property of her husband.

End of the knights......................

Knights and their castles became much less significant towards the end of the Middle Ages, and towns grew in size and importance. At the same time, knights were becoming less important on the battlefield as foot soldiers began to play a more important role in warfare.

Full-time army

From the 14th century, kings began to hire trained soldiers called mercenaries to fight for them, instead of knights. Unlike knights, these new soldiers worked all year round and were paid wages. Some knights still fought for their king, but many preferred to stay at home and look after their estates instead.

Longbows and pikes

As early as 1300, knights had begun to lose their advantage on the battlefield. Powerful longbows were developed that could fire arrows right through armour. Meanwhile, foot soldiers began to use new tactics. For example, they formed walls of deadly spikes by standing close together and pointing their pikes and halberds outwards. This forced knights to get off their horses and fight on foot.

These longbowmen stand ready to fire over the heads of their fellow soldiers and into the midst of the enemy.

Changing castles

By the late Middle Ages, the use of cannons had become common in siege warfare. Traditional castles were not designed to stand up to such powerful weapons, so people began to build new kinds of castles, called artillery forts, or gun forts.

Gun forts were built for defence and not as homes, although they did provide basic living quarters for a garrison of soldiers. They had low, wide walls which made them very difficult to destroy, and they were designed so that it was easy to fire cannons and guns out of them.

Deal Castle is an example of an early gun fort. The raised areas, called gun platforms, made it easier to fire cannons and guns at the enemy.

The rise of merchants

In the towns, merchants became increasingly wealthy and powerful. Merchants were tradesmen who made money by buying and selling goods, especially luxury ones, from abroad. Kings began to look to merchants, rather than to knights, for financial and political support, and eventually, even began to knight them. This was seen as an honorary title rather than a military one, and these new knights were not expected to fight.

Medieval merchants bought and sold their goods in markets like the one shown here.

Fact: In some countries, people are still knighted today as a reward for services to their country.

41

Famous knights

Many knights became well known for their exploits. Here you can read about some of the most famous ones.

Godfrey de Bouillon, a French knight, was among the first knights who went to fight in the First Crusade. He had to sell much of his land to pay for his journey to the Holy Land. After Jerusalem was conquered by the crusaders in 1099, he became its king, but was killed in battle the following year.

This is the coat of arms Godfrey de Bouillon had while he was king of Jerusalem.

Bertrand du Guesclin was one of the most famous French knights of his time. He fought in many battles during the Hundred Years' War between England and France. He was an outstanding military leader. Under his command the French recaptured much of the land that the English had taken from them.

This medieval painting shows Bertrand du Guesclin leading an attack on the town of Pestien, in France.

Rodrigo de Vivar was a Spanish knight who at different times in his career fought both for the Christians and the Muslims. He was nicknamed "El Cid", which means "the lord", by his admiring soldiers. He is famous for having never lost a battle.

William Marshal had many victories on the tournament field and fought with the Templars in the Holy Land. He served in the court of three English kings and was ambassador for England. King Richard I gave William enough land and castles to make him one of the most powerful nobles in the country.

Boucicaut, a French knight, became a soldier at a young age, showing great skill in battle at just 16. He was the founder of the order of the White Lady of the Green Shield, whose members all swore to protect defenceless noblewomen.

Prince Edward (the Black Prince) was an English knight who was much feared by his enemies because he was such a good commander in battle. Under his command, 7,000 English soldiers defeated 18,000 French soldiers at the Battle of Poitiers, in 1356. He was probably called the Black Prince because he always wore black armour.

This statue of Richard I shows him about to lead a battle charge.

This bronze statue of the Black Prince is from his grave in Canterbury Cathedral, in England.

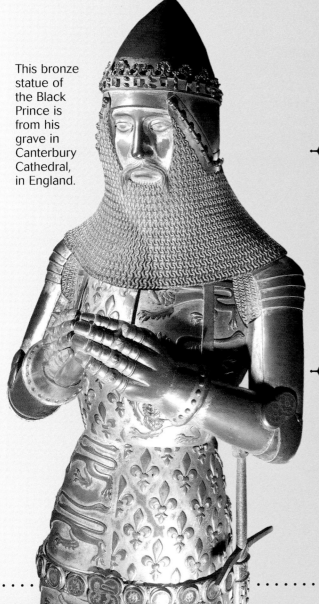

King Richard I of England was known as "Richard the lionheart" because of his bravery and skill on the battlefield. He spent most of his reign fighting abroad in the Third Crusade, and against the King of France. In fact, he only spent six months out of his ten-year reign in England. His adventures as a knight came to an end when he died of an infected wound he had received during a siege.

Simon de Montfort of France is famous for his ruthless persecution of a group of people called Albigensians. They were heretics (people who disagreed with some of the teachings of the church). De Montfort led an army in a crusade against them, destroying castles, ransacking towns and killing thousands of men, women and children.

Knight facts

Life as a knight was varied and action-packed. Here are some fascinating facts about what they got up to, both on and off the battlefield.

— During his campaigns against Scotland and Wales, King Edward I of England had to ban tournaments, because his knights kept going off to fight in them when they were needed to fight in real battles.

— Wooden siege engines were often covered with animal skins that had been soaked in vinegar or urine to prevent them from catching fire.

— In peacetime, army commanders occasionally used trebuchets to fling flowers and petals at ladies who were watching tournaments.

— The French knight Boucicaut was said to have been able to jump onto his horse and to turn a somersault in a full suit of armour.

— Even with the help of a squire, it could take a knight up to an hour to get dressed in a complete suit of plate armour.

— During lengthy sieges, knights sometimes held tournaments with the enemy to relieve the boredom.

— While the French town of Calais was under siege, in 1346, a small temporary town, with houses, shops and a marketplace, was built outside the walls, so that the soldiers could await their enemy's surrender in comfort.

— In most tournament competitions, knights tried to avoid hurting each other badly. During jousts, for example, they used blunt-tipped lances which could not pierce armour.

These men are jousting with blunt-tipped lances. They also wear extra armour on the side of the body that's most likely to be hit.

—— Up to six different types of craftsmen worked together to make a 14th-century suit of plate armour. Hammerers moulded the plates to fit the knight, locksmiths made hinges, mailmakers made chain mail to cover the knight's joints, millmen polished the armour, and engravers and etchers decorated it.

—— Very large war horses were specially bred for knights to fight on. They weighed about twice as much as ordinary horses.

—— Sometimes, when knights' war horses had their shoes put on, sharp nail heads were left sticking out of them to injure foot soldiers who got in their way.

—— In 1212, thousands of children set off on a crusade to the Holy Land. None of them ever reached the Holy Land and very few returned home. Many were killed, and others were captured and sold as slaves.

—— In the 14th and 15th centuries, Italy was one of the main centres for armour-making. Whole villages were employed to produce suits of armour as quickly as possible.

—— At tournaments, ladies sometimes gave knights a scarf or ribbon to wear while they were competing. By wearing a lady's scarf, a knight showed that he was dedicating his performance in the tournament to her.

—— More soldiers died from disease during the Crusades than from injuries received in battle.

—— During sieges, attacking armies sometimes used trebuchets to toss the severed heads of enemy soldiers or messengers back into their own castle.

Acknowledgements......................

Every effort has been made to trace the copyright holders of the material in this book. If any rights have been omitted, the publishers offer to rectify this in any subsequent editions following notification. The publishers are grateful to the following organizations and individuals for their permission to reproduce material (t=top, m=middle, b=bottom, l=left, r=right):

Cover Photograph by Neil Francis, with special thanks to Arms and Archery; **p1** © Archivo Iconografico, S.A./CORBIS; **p2–3** © Archivo Iconografico, S.A./CORBIS; **p4** © The Board of the Trustees of the Armouries; **p5** (tl) © The Board of the Trustees of the Armouries, (tm) © The Art Archive/Album/Joseph Martin, (tr) © Cadw: Welsh Heritage Monuments Crown Copyright (b) © Bibliothèque Nationale, Paris, France/Bridgeman Art Library; **p7** (bl), (m) and (br) Photos of medieval weapons courtesy of Global Outlet, 3324 N. Harlem Ave., Chicago, Illinois 60634, U.S.A., (r) Digital Artwork Image © Skip Moore; **p8** (r) Photograph courtesy of Christian H. Tobler, (bl) © The Board of the Trustees of the Armouries; **p9** (t) © Nik Wheeler/CORBIS, (br) © Charles & Josette Lenars/CORBIS; **p10** © Philadelphia Museum of Art/CORBIS; **p11** © Christie's Images, Inc./Christie's Images. All rights reserved; **p12–13** © Derek Croucher/CORBIS; **p14–15** © The Malcolm Group Events Limited, Herstmonceux Castle Medieval Festival, background © Ted Spiegel/CORBIS, background © Raymond Gehman/CORBIS; **p18** © Chris Hellier/CORBIS; **p19** Crown Copyright reproduced courtesy of Historic Scotland; **p21** Photograph courtesy of Dr. John Goodall; **p23** (br) © The British Library/Heritage-Images; **p24** © Pete Dancs/Getty Images; **p25** (tl) © Archivo Iconografico, S.A./CORBIS; **p28** (tr) © Mary Evans Picture Library; **p29** (ml) © Philadelphia Museum of Art/CORBIS, (br) © By permission of the British Library, add. 38537 f29.; **p30** © The Art Archive/Bibliothèque Nationale Paris/Harper Collins Publishers; **p31** (bl) and (bm) © National Museums of Scotland/Bridgeman Art Library, (br) © Biblioteca Monasterio del Escorial, Madrid, Spain/Bridgeman Art Library; **p32** (m) The British Museum/Bridgeman Art Library, (br) © Mary Evans Picture Library; **p33** The Art Archive/Musée Condé Chantilly/Dagli Orti; **p34** © The Art Archive/British Library/British Library; **p36–37** © Arthur Thévenart/CORBIS; **p36** (tr) © The Master and Fellows of Corpus Christi College, Cambridge; **p37** (tl) Photo courtesy of the Brotherhood of Blessed Gérard, (ml) Photograph reproduced with the kind permission of The Museum of the Order of St. John, St. John Ambulance, (mr) © Order of St. John; **p38** (tr) © The Art Archive/Musée Condé Chantilly/The Art Archive, (bl) © The Art Archive/Castello di Manta Asti/Dagli Orti (A); **p39** (tr) © Archivo Iconografico, S.A./CORBIS, (b) © Historical Picture Archive/CORBIS; **p40** © Archivo Iconografico, S.A./CORBIS; **p41** (m) © English Heritage/Heritage-Images, (b) © Historical Picture Archive/CORBIS; **p42** (b) © The British Library/Heritage-Images; **p43** (tr) © Angelo Hornak/CORBIS, (l) © The Art Archive/Canterbury Cathedral/Eileen Tweedy; **p44–45** © Patrick Ward/CORBIS

We would also like to thank English Heritage for use of their pictures on pages 6 (l) and (r) and 26 (tl).

English Heritage is the independent but government-sponsored body responsible for the historic environment of England. Its aim is to protect England's unique architectural and archaeological heritage for the benefit and enjoyment of future generations. English Heritage cares for over 400 sites, from Stonehenge and Hadrian's Wall, to dozens of medieval castles and abbeys. English Heritage has a large events programme covering popular favourites, such as outdoor concerts with fireworks, garden talks, tours and shows, battle re-enactments, jousting and falconry, music and dance, outdoor theatre and festivals for children. Full details are contained in a free Events diary, available from English Heritage's customer services department. English Heritage currently has around 470,000 members. Joining enables you to visit all the sites absolutely free, while supporting their work. To find out more, or to join, please contact English Heritage Customer Services Department, PO Box 570, Swindon SN2 2UR, telephone 0870 333 1182, or e-mail members@english-heritage.org.uk. A catalogue of publications is also available from the same address, or by e-mailing customers@english-heritage.org.uk

Managing designer: Mary Cartwright.
Photographic manipulation: Mike Wheatley. Picture researcher: Ruth King.
With many thanks to Susanna Davidson, Neil Francis, Abigail Wheatley and Alice Pearcey.

Usborne Publishing is not responsible and does not accept liability for the availability or content of any Web site other than its own, or for any exposure to harmful, offensive, or inaccurate material which may appear on the Web. Usborne Publishing will have no liability for any damage or loss caused by viruses that may be downloaded as a result of browsing the sites it recommends. Usborne downloadable pictures are the copyright of Usborne Publishing Ltd and may not be reproduced in print or in electronic form for any commercial or profit-related purpose.

First published in 2003 by Usborne Publishing Ltd, 83-85 Saffron Hill, London EC1N 8RT. www.usborne.com
Copyright © 2003 Usborne Publishing Ltd. The name Usborne and the devices ⊕♀ are Trade Marks of Usborne Publishing Ltd. All rights reserved. No part of this publication may be reproduced, stored in a retrieval system, or transmitted in any form or by any means, electronic, mechanical, photocopying, recording or otherwise, without the prior permission of the publisher. Printed in Portugal.

Using the Internet

Most of the Web sites described in this book can be accessed with a standard home computer and a Web browser (the software that enables you to display information from the Internet). We recommend:

- A PC with Microsoft® Windows® 98 or later version, or a Macintosh computer with System 9.0 or later, and 64Mb RAM
- A browser such as Microsoft® Internet Explorer 5, or Netscape® 6, or later versions
- Connection to the Internet via a modem (preferably 56Kbps) or a faster digital or cable line
- An account with an Internet Service Provider (ISP)
- A sound card to hear sound files

Extras

Some Web sites need additional programs, called plug-ins, to play sounds, or to show videos, animations or 3-D images. If you go to a site and you do not have the necessary plug-in, a message saying so will come up on the screen. There is usually a button on the site that you can click on to download the plug-in. Alternatively, go to **www.usborne-quicklinks.com** and click on **Net Help**. There you can find links to download plug-ins. Here is a list of plug-ins you might need:

RealPlayer® – lets you play videos and hear sound files.
QuickTime – enables you to view video clips.
Shockwave® – lets you play animations and interactive programs.
Flash™ – lets you play animations.

Help

For general help and advice on using the Internet, go to **Usborne Quicklinks** at **www.usborne-quicklinks.com** and click on **Net Help**. To find out more about how to use your Web browser, click on **Help** at the top of the browser and then choose **Contents and Index**. You'll find a huge searchable dictionary containing tips on how to find your way around the Internet easily.

Internet safety

Remember to follow the Internet safety guidelines at the front of this book. For more safety information, go to **Usborne Quicklinks** and click on **Net Help**.

Computer viruses

A computer virus is a program that can seriously damage your computer. A virus can get into your computer when you download programs from the Internet, or in an attachment (an extra file) that arrives with an e-mail. We strongly recommend that you buy anti-virus software to protect your computer, and that you update the software regularly.

Internet link

For links to Web sites where you can find out more about computer viruses, go to **www.usborne-quicklinks.com** and click on Net Help.

Macintosh and QuickTime are trademarks of Apple Computer, Inc., registered in the U.S. and other countries.
RealPlayer is a trademark of RealNetworks, Inc., registered in the U.S. and other countries.
Flash and Shockwave are trademarks of Macromedia, Inc., registered in the U.S. and other countries.

Index